Dom

Hope you enjoy
this book

Geo.

# MY LIFE
# IN PIECES

## By Andrew Horner

*The front cover for the book is designed by Michael Felton.*

# ACKNOWLEDGEMENTS

*Thank you so much to my family!*

*Anne & John – for all your constant love and support and encouragement and looking over every word I've ever written. You're the best Mum and Dad in the world.*

*Sara - my incredible wife and co-pilot through life thank you for being there every step of the way.*

*Douglas - for inspiring me to read and write more and inspiring my poetry through music. Thank you, brother.*

*Janice - for reading so many of my pieces, even though you secretly wished more of them were Haikus.*

*Michael - thank you for joining me on this crazy ride. Creating such beautiful artwork. @squarespecs*

# INTRO

'My Life in Pieces' is a semi-auto biographical account of my life through poems and the way I have seen the world change during some of these challenging times. This book is aimed at people dealing with mental health issues, depression and anxiety. Especially over the last few years. *When the world went crazy, art kept me sane.*

I would describe my work as raw, relevant, and thought provoking. The pieces I have written deal with the complexities of the human mind and how we all must fight our unwanted demons in whatever form they manifest themselves. These poems I hope can inspire change, open conversations on tough topics but most importantly be relatable moments that can touch other souls.

They always have an uplifting quality no matter how dark the journey a lot of the pieces are themed around this ever-changing world, social media addiction, phone addiction, mental health, suicide awareness, love and loss and the power of healing oneself.

I think this book can help in creating conversations about things society deems taboo. It may even help people to see the world in another way. Words can do so much not only to help the individual to empower themselves but can also help them find their own truth.

This book is about changing the narrative. To be vulnerable is actually a strength not a weakness. For far too long, men have had to hide away their emotions from the eyes of society and I believe that does more damage in the long run and can lead to mental health, break downs and perhaps even suicide all the dark things we go through in life are lessons that make us stronger and bring us in touch with our souls, allowing us to tap into our true spiritual side. Life isn't an easy ride for any of us, it's okay if you feel like you're going to break sometimes. As long as you can find a way back to those missing pieces you can be whole again.

With its many micro poems and longer pieces this book will be a refreshing break from social media and hopefully a warm embrace of encouraging words showing people out there that they are not alone. If these words can help just one person, then that's the greatest gift.

This is a poetry book that deals with mental health, suicide awareness, love, loss and the power of healing oneself. It's an attempt to break the social stigma around men and their emotions as it can be difficult for men to express their feelings and emotions, let alone write them into poetry and prose.
I'm hoping this book can get men to 'open up' and allow them the freedom to express their emotions and not hide away under that toxic phrase 'Man up'.

A lot of my poems and prose have a deeper and more profound nature to them, echoing inspiration from the likes of Paulo Coelho and some of his books 'The Warrior of light' and 'The Alchemist'.

'My Life in Pieces' is a collection of poetry and prose about the human condition and the complex world we find ourselves in. It is moments and extracts from my time dealing with my mental health and the cathartic nature of words and writing your feelings.

This book can allow people to get away from all the noise and speed of this crazy world and just take some time to breathe, reflect and hopefully even heal.

When you are in your darkest moments thinking you're going through it alone, this book is a friend to remind you that you're not alone.

I hope it can be an inspiration from one *warrior of light* to another.


For more poems, artwork and projects...
Check out @Talesofthenook on Instagram.

# TABLE OF CONTENTS

# POEMS ABOUT LIFE

# CRACKED

I tried to crack the silence to see if it would break.
So I could take a tiny piece as a keepsake.
Now I'm drowning in all the noise.
As I contemplate on my mistake.
Silence is bliss.
It's the overbearing noise of this world.
I cannot take.

# MOTH

Don't you just feel
Like a moth?
On a cold winter walk alone.
When you see a light on inside a stranger's home.

All you want is to be inside cosy and safe.
In that golden warm embrace.

# LADYBIRD

Watching your last moments
As you struggle
Breaks every part of me.

Your beautiful shell
Still intact
Time up
Your life is extracted.

So delicate and beautiful
There as you lie.

It's so hard to watch a ladybird die.

# FALLING LEAVES

I thought my life was so important
My **problems** were as big as mountains
My **pains** were as deep as oceans
My **love** was as damaged as the rain forests
My **mind** trapped like people trying to flee from war torn
countries and misery.

But in the grand scheme of things, we're nothing but **leaves** in
the wind.

# CAUGHT ONLINE

We're caught in a labyrinth the candy store
With no age limit
They cater for all as our data falls
Into the puppeteers' lap
Manipulating our every move
Planned out, our future blueprint map
Humans are now the new lab rats
Advertising companies creating rabbit holes.
To capitalise with ease.
There's plenty of fish in the sea.
We are the fish now that struggle to break free.
Caught online. Their line.
Specially designed by incredible minds.
Selling our souls and killing our time.
Human bait, dopamine snacks.
Our minds and wallets have been hijacked.
Addicted to that black hole, that erodes our soul.
Stealing away our attention with its innocent blue glow.
But let's not forget behind all those likes and follows
There are so many young people that won't see a tomorrow.
Lives taken from families every day.
Killed by the vulgar popularity game we all play.
Bullying that doesn't stop in the playground.
It follows you back home.
A cluster bomb disguised as an innocent post on your phone.
Toxic words erode the damaged souls that are left on their own.

# A SOCIAL DISTANCE
# FROM SOCIAL MEDIA

I had a wonderful conversation today.
With an old man in the park.
Putting the world to rights
Sat two meters apart.
So many people stood upright
Like giraffes their necks so tall
No one around for miles
Were able to stare at their phones and scroll.
Refreshing to see the whites of his eyes.
No blue light across his face.
We were both in the real world.
Both fully present in that place.
Happy in each other's company.
Our minds were set free
From our subconscious prison
We're trapped in daily.
Searching for dopamine's.
Like, fishermen scowering the sea.
Not hunched over our phones
Like birds of prey.
I'll always remember the way I felt.
The internet died that day.

# FREE DOOM

Hold on tightly
Freedom asked.
Held hostage by secret plans
They have yet to pass
Clenched safely between our palms.
We must all keep you safe from harm.
Hold on tightly through the heavy winds that pass.
If you open up to check on me
I'll be taken away in a gust you see.
Stolen away and none shall be free.
As technology grows
Our minds shrink
They control our minds and wallets now
We've all forgotten how to think
Broken into particles of dust
Stop, think and look up ahead
We're fat and fatigued by the breadcrumbs we've all been fed.
Dogs on a government leash as we're being so easily led.
As we watch our freedom fall.
The world they want for us.
Won't be fun at all.
Hold on tight.

# HOT TOPIC

The little boy
Who grew up setting ants ablaze
Under the suns magnificent gaze.
Chopping heads off plants
Scuffing up the grass.
Making boats out of empty plastic bottles.
Inspired by his destruction as he laughs.
The world now burns.
Trees for miles
Lit like candles.
While all the while.
Ice breaks and melts.
The sea rises like an angry snake.
The winters are strangely warm.
The weather is angry and bizarre.
I feel the pandemic of anxiety crashing like a wave
We've pushed our beautiful planet too far.

# WE'RE NOT BROKEN

Pain is the chain
That links us all.
Like lightning strikes our hearts
Scared to trust again
In case we fall.
Frightened by our damaged parts.
Scattered into a million pieces
We can glue them back together with gold.
The scars we wear now
Remind the others
We're not that easy to fool.

# HEADS OR TALES?

You stirred my mind
Like a soup flavoured from a thousand voices over time
Echoing In unison, like a chorus leading the blind.
Yet I'm left behind.
Voices like harsh rocks smashing windows in abandoned homes.
Crack dens laced with holes for broken souls.
That's where happy thoughts are murderer.
A crime scene for what could have been.
The mean thoughts that bully the good.
Like gangsters who own that hood.
Or ghost Like creeps that would murder children in the woods.
The dark forest that resides behind the blacks of our eyes
The muffled screams from our inner child trapped inside.
That's what darkness feels like.
Not a canvas stained black as night.
Thoughts that perhaps wanted to be something else.
But got caught in the wrong crowd.
A plague that spreads across our subconscious ground.
Where pieces of hope are shattered and scattered and lost.
But desperately hoping to catch that train of thought so they
can be found.
Muted by the demonic versions
As they fight to find their sound.
The diamonds among our rough.
In amongst all our painful stuff.
Maybe pain is our love that got twisted around?
Healing that's confused as its inside out.
That blanket of joy that just got stuck.
On the thorns of fear that tear through the fabric of you.

As those best parts sadly disappear.
We stare in the mirror hoping they'll reappear.
Like a delayed magic trick.
The kind that makes your mind sick.
Sharp thoughts cutting at your flesh.
Like a fine red line.
That cries from inside.
A darkness that thirsts for those metallic tears
Craving a taste for our innocence and deep essence.
As we become Landlords
To the band of demons who are now our tenants
That club together, to break our hearts.
Bury our diamonds with their spades.
Because that's the hands we were dealt.
Sadly, our thoughts make it that way.
But let's take a rain check
As we reshuffle the deck.
We can clean these dirty hands.
And start a fresh.
These cards maybe touched by darkness.
But we can still see their true value
Their suit.
Which suits me just fine.
Where there is dark there is light.
In the storm of our mind
Hope is that silver line.
Stars remind us of this constant fight.
As they pierce their way through the dark of night.
Like fragmented pieces of broken glass.
Or sparkling glowing ninja stars that barely last.
That is the battle for all of us.
We're both sides of that coin toss.
The dull scratched unreadable heads.
Yet we have shiny bright new pristine tales ahead of us.
You are not measured by how liquid your wallet is.

Or how many amazing kids.
Or the acres of the land where you live.
Or the amazing job that you did.
It's what you can bring to this world.
And what you can truly give.
Time is the only currency there is
Spend it wisely
Because there are no refunds on this.

# HEAVY ARE THE YOUNG

I discovered the meaning of self-love
Not from a book or audio tape
Or from way above.
It was deep inside me.
Born out of self-reflection.
Enough was enough
The gloves are off
Time to delve into some complex stuff.
Love isn't always wine and roses
It corrodes parts of your life like acid.
Heart breaking music that the heart composes.
In lockdown I was blown away
Like the bullets sprayed from young kids of today.
Forced to be gangsters not sure what path to take
As they are too afraid, caught in the youthful traps of today.
Surviving for respect as they lost their way.
How can people still be murdered and kidnapped during the
day?
Is this the way humans deal with a crisis?
Creating more death and chaos just to pull through this.
Because that's all we know.
It's time to let that go.
Hasn't this virus taken enough good souls?
We're human spirits that desperately need to grow.
It's lockdown.
These kids stab each other over an invisible crown.
To become the king of a crumbling town.
As their respect and brothers leave them
Like a house of cards comes crashing down.

Post code wars
Fighting with blades instead of swords.
But what's all this death really for?
Their dates are shocking on their headstones.
Their futures gone, not even postponed.
Empty beds in their parents' homes.
The streets turning into killing zones.
Their music video hits a thousand more views
On their smart phones.
Never even made a dent on their student loans.
It doesn't make sense
We're the ones that make our lives more intense.
Someone pressed the crazy button long ago.
We wait in the wings with suspense.
How do we stop all this non-sense?
And help create change?
Stopping the dark wave that rips through our world.
Making its way to the front page.
The newsroom
Awash with doom
Souls trapped inside
Choking on gloom.
Our only way to each other is now through Zoom.
As I close the chapter on this book
And pray for a new.
If they lack the love from a home
They look elsewhere for it.
If we don't let them tell their story
They'll damage their own world.
The reason they take lives so easily
Is because they don't understand the value of a life.
They don't respect life, love and peace.
All they know is trying to survive on the streets.
To all those lost souls from turbulent homes
Anger and confusion turn to poison

Flowing through their veins.
Young lives being snubbed out like flames.
The frightening truth of toxic masculinity.
A dangerous lesson, for their harsh reality.

# HANDCUFFS

Generation x
Have had to contend with such complex events
Anxiety and stress dialled up to madness
Overwhelming expectations to constantly impress
Hard to jump hurdles and be your best
Life's a complex puzzle designed to test
Touch screens
More than you can touch skin
Masking up
Words distorted from within.
Pains and feeling are allowed to be expressed
It's not a sin.
So hard to feel the light
When too many get comfortable in the dark
A generation that needs to explore
Thumbs aren't as important as your hearts
Where social media ends, your lives start
Mobiles are handcuffs
A doorway to some dangerous stuff
Complex and destructive things
A temptation that can clip your wings.
Life isn't something you scroll through
It has to be lived in.

# CELEBRITY

I make my millions
Taking on the wrath of being a celebrity
Spending most of my money
Yoyoing throughout therapy.

You celebrate my life
As I look at yours with envy.
You can't quiet see
*Normal* no longer exists for me.

It's now a media frenzy
I'm up on the big screen or on your TV.
You think that gives you the right to my home life and privacy?

I spill my soul on camera for all to see.
But that's not enough for you lot?
My long list of pain
Is my autobiography.

You know everything about me
There's nothing to hide behind
When you're a celebrity.

# DIGITAL DIRT

You are never alone
Now that you have a phone.
A window to view over a million souls
When you're lost you can escape into that zone.
But what happens when it's gone?
When that social fix is unplugged and that lifeline comes un
done.
A support machine you can no longer depend on.
And it suddenly dawns on you
that it's like being starved of oxygen.
Can we live without it being on?
Burning a hole in our pockets
To see if we've been missed or messaged by anyone.
It's great that there Is a place to escape.
But what happens when that space becomes a mind cage?
That sabotages our brains
As we inject each other's feeds with hearts that we trade.
That let so many souls connect
And even the darker ones misbehave.
Behind the scenes
In DM rooms where they can't be seen.
Conflicted conversations that cause a scene.
Innocent lives, emojis and memes.
But what about those sprinkles of darkness in-between?
Not all the minds on social media are clean.

# DUST

It gathers around the house.
Stacked in all the corners.
You might not see that if you're homeless.
It's along the pavements instead.
Blowing up into people's faces.
As we watch the passers-by.
Skating across the ground with the leaves.
Or up, up into the sky.
Twinkling there like fool's gold.
You can write your name in dust so I'm told.
Helping you out with your spelling.
It's particles of us, our own skin.
Just as a snake shedding.
When we come to the end of our lives.
We are all grains of dust.
Dancing through the air or mixed into sand from a gust.
Or swimming out amongst fishes deep in the sea.
Or perhaps we'll be in an urn on a shelf.
Watching other dust around us.
I guess we'll have to wait and see.

# CONFUSED SHEPHERD'S

Sky blazing orange.
Like it's our iconic sci-fi fill.
Blade runner.
Feels like our species must run or this virus makes us ill.
Running from a sharp blade.
It's their sharp lies.
They'd sewn up our eyes with technology.
Like a magician creates miss direction.
To pull off their trick.
But the planet crying out to us that it's sick.

Bloody palms, sky like napalm.
Can barely breath through these masks.
Trying hard to focus and just stay calm.
But how about some smoke to go in those lungs.
Watching TV away from all the harm.
Whilst homes are barbequed by the sun.
Is this the world we leave behind for some?
People thinking, we gave it our all.
Is this the world trying to tell us something?
Perhaps our final call?
We all know "Red sky at night" right?
But what is orange sky during the day?
Stay away?
From the dismay.

Is it too late to turn things around?
Is this our sins left for our children to pay?
The price for the lies and things we let slide.

No longer anywhere left we can hide.
Landslides, fires changing the skies.
War and famine, no more drugs to kill the time.
Oxygen sold on Amazon for a bargain price.
Next day delivery if you go with Prime.

Dropped off by drones in the blink of an eye.
It'll only cost you a lung or two.
As the world turns orange our faces still remain blue.
It's time to put our phones away.
Face our addictions and fears.
Embrace our vulnerability and allow those tears.
There are no superhero's here.
We need to face up to the truth and make the change.
Before our beautiful world may disappear.

# LESSONS FROM LIFE

Never really learnt at school
As I was too busy acting the fool.
Always finding an excuse for being a jerk
Any opportunity to run far away from work.
Kissing in library's never appreciating books
Chased girls far out of my league
Blinded by their looks.
But as I age and embrace my greys
I realise that we're given lessons
Every single day.

Our darkness is a classroom with no lights on.
But the lessons there are truly enlightening.

# MOBILITUS

This is the disease we don't talk about.
The dangerous new trend.
I can no longer use my hands
A mobile it stuck to the other end.

I take you for a walk
Or when I go out to see friends.
You interrupt me during movies
It was an infatuation that now must end.
I'm checking you when I'm driving
Or when I'm on a date.
My hot food turning cold abandoned on the plate.

Will they bury us together in my coffin?
Is that what it will take?
How about we make some kind of deal?
I need to start to experience life for real.
And give my poor hands a rest.
I've got to stop being out of this world.
When being in it is best.

# NEVER KNOWING

We wake. We cry. We're loved. We try.
We grow.
We spiral. We trip.
We fall.
We quake. We crawl. We stand tall. We fight.

We love.
We lose.
We win. We're brave. We're light. We're dark. We age.

We break.
We die.
We rise.
We live in their hearts and minds. We are forever.

Every day that comes.
As we dive into the unknown together.

# WHERE DO WE GO?

Where do we go?
When life gets hard.
Where do we go?
When your surrounded by demons with a dull sword.
Where do we go?
When we feel invisible and just ignored.
Where do we go?
When the rain of negativity hits every part of your being.
Where do we go?
When you are over feeling.
Where do you go?
When you lack the ability to be human.
Where do you go?
When the lights go out.
Where do you go?
When the crowd of judging voice's start to shout.
Where do you go?
When the moon starts to bleed.
Where do you go?
When the stars can no longer be seen.
Where do you go?
When the pain and confusion of life makes it too hard to
breath.
Where do you go?
When the air is no longer clean.
Where do you go?
When you've seen all that can be seen.
Where do you go?
When the horrors are the only thing, they show.

Where do we go?
When we fall on hard times.
Where do we go?
When we can no longer say we're fine.
Where do we go?
When it's our time.
Where do we go?
When hope seems so low.
Where do we go?
When we crave a yes but get showered with nos.
Where do we go?
To collect our broken mess.
Where do we go?
When we have nothing left.
Where do we go?

# WHAT IF?

What if you're the mess in that immaculate place?
What if you're the claustrophobia in that expansive space?
What if you're that taste of poison that makes your heart race?
What if you're the calling card for the demons to give chase?
What if you're the missing words on a wall that's been defaced?
What if you're the blame when somebodies been misplaced?
What if you're the darkness that you're too afraid to face?
What if you're the list that tallies up all those mistakes?
What if you're the stain that others tried to erase?
What if you're that bad friend in the mirror that you need to replace?
What if a lick of fresh paint doesn't change the place?
What if you're the party that stays out late?
What if you're the cracks in that broken china plate?
What if you're the bad influence that's waiting by the gate?
What if you're the wrong when everything's right?
What if you're that fear that keeps you awake at night?
What if you're work is needed deep within?
What if the storm isn't above, you but it's under your skin?
What if the answers aren't at the end of a getaway?
What if the truth to set you free has been with you every day?
What if you stop your mind from constantly thinking?
And discover in you is the power of healing.
What if...you stop saying all those *what ifs?*
And go out into the world and start to live.

# TRAFFIC LIGHTS

I've ransacked every library there is to find the book on life.
Without it I feel like I have no spine keeping me upright.
But we're aloud to fall along the way.
Learning from every cut and scar now on display.
Every inch of pain are the hidden words we were unable to say.
We can all get overwhelmed by the traffic building up in our
mind's motorway.
Some thoughts are out to cause a crash speeding ahead without
giving-way.
It's all green lights up ahead,
A red one occasionally just to calm my nerves
Time to reflect on all those lessons I wrote down
But sadly the ones I've never read.
In life you either win or learn,
You only lose, if you let those lessons go up in flames
And sit back and just watch them burn.

# THE FILTER SYSTEM

I stare at the screen.
Positioning myself just right.
The perfect angle.
My flaws hidden out of sight.
With the flick of a finger.
As the technology genie gives me my wish.
Take away all my imperfections.
My anxiety list.
A filter here, a filter there.
I know longer recognise myself.
But as long as I get those likes, who cares.
Why do we hide behind these layers?
Too afraid to be ourselves.
All the things that make me, me.
Hidden behind layers to protect our fragility.
Skin as smooth as silk.
Now wrinkle free.
Bags under the eyes disappear magically.
No longer the person I recognise.
Feeling more like a celebrity.
This imposter on my screen in front of my eye.
Everything unique and human erased.
Like someone plucked all the stars from the night sky.
Ironic we call these photos a selfie
As it doesn't resemble any of me.
It's sad we live in a world, where we can't grow old gracefully.

# THE MISSING

I can see all the red, so perfectly
No shapes or figures hiding it from me.
Lights collecting particles of dust.
No audience's hubbub or people making a fuss.
Feeling the huge absence.
As do all of us.
The gaping hole in sight.
Wings now empty.
Costumes hung like witches, that failed to take flight.
The stage pitch black
Except for the tiny beams of light through all the cracks.
Rats in the walls
No longer disturbed by humans at all.
Wigs left upon the shelf.
Art put on pause for people's health.
Artists restless in their homes.
Unsure of their futures
Sealed off by this virus that now roams.
Props boxed up, like someone's moving away.
No front of house
A box office with nothing on display.
Eerie silence dominates
This empty shell of a place.
Once a vibrant world, filling our imagination
Now an abandoned space.
A sea of red seats all missing a face.

# SKIN & BONE

Hollywood.
Now just humans and trees.
An empty wood.
The land of make believe.
Confused of how we mistake these super stars for human beings.
A virus reminded us.
It doesn't matter how much money we own.
Or how big and luxurious our home.
We all need to breath and survive.
There is a dived line, between those that can live.
And those that can barely survive.
As a woman dies of starvation next to her new-born baby.
We're upset about our restaurant bills.
This world has just gone crazy
Superhero's on the big screen.
Struggling to organise lessons for their kids daily.
Children picking out a face mask they love.
That can dilute this danger.
Something fun and exciting for this new world
That's now become so much stranger.
The new world where boundaries are set.
Beyond the terrorism and world wars there is a new threat.
Feeling like we're all staring in a new apocalyptic film.
Except the title is called reality.
Now trapped inside the latest episode of Black Mirrors.
So, life like its practically now 4D.
It's food and clean air we crave.
Not boat loads of money.
When the last tree falls

None of us are free.
We're just leaves in the wind.
Skin and bone.
Fighting to create positive change.
On this big planet we all call home.

# POEMS ABOUT LOVE

# WHAT IS LOVE?

Love is the wind kissing the trees.
Love is flowers slow dancing with bees.
Love is kind gestures that bring others to their knees.
Love is putting someone else first before your own needs.
Love is kissing flaws and rough edges from one's skin.
Love is accepting each other with the pains they bare deep within.
Love is protecting each other's dreams when demons are at bay.
Love is the answer when you have clearly lost your way.
Love is listening with eyes and ears.
Love is hearing their heart sing for years and years.
Love is the strength to lift someone after a million tears.
Love is being you without the fear.
Love is the invisible bridge linking all living things.
Love is the most powerful energy we all can bring.

# MIRROR ME

What do you see in your reflection?
Beyond your flaws and imperfections.
You are pure magic if you just pay close attention.
Can we all find kindness for ourselves
Beyond this built-up aggression.
Love yourself first before you can love others
Was a truly important lesson.
You are what you see first in the morning,
So why not make a good first impression.
What are you waiting for?
You don't need to ask for your own permission.
Self-love and being kind is your only mission.
There are two sides to us.
One is true and the other is fiction.
One that truly exists the one we make believe in.
But we are losing faith in our own skin.
Now our mirrors have become like scalpels as we dissect every tiny thing.

That becomes larger than life.
Until it eventually takes over
We can no longer see who we are
We are in the shadow of our other.
We've forgotten how to trust ourselves.
And our emotions you see.
We're all stuck behind these bright colourful emojis.
But these animated pieces we choose to use
To share the feelings and emotions that are no longer being used.

Has got us all confused.
Throwing our emotions to the curb as they feel obsolete
We can toss in a cartoon feeling to express our day
Or a gif that's a random moment on repeat.
Why not find the true you in that moment?
The one that's impossible to beat.
But a true gift is being yourself in any given situation.
Even when you're fighting the urge to retreat.

There are so many amazing parts to all of us
That we abandoned along the way.
Like children that outgrow their toys
The broken ones that are now tarnished and old
Are no longer on display
Thrown into a box with the other lot
The ones that don't get to play.
But what does this say?
About us today?
When something is damaged, do we just cast it away?
It's fine, the new upgrade has better features and a cooler face
anyway.
Pissed off now, as we have to wait.
Maybe that's why we struggle as a human race.
We care too much about what people think of us in the first
place.

Those parts of us we feel we have lost
The parts we used to love, but can no longer trust
Like old toys discarded in a box sat around now collecting dust
Sat on the ground with all these dark thoughts gathered around
Like I'm at an AA meeting for the mind.
Those parts of us that now dictate our worlds from the inside.
Our flaws should be the stars that stop us in our tracks with
wonder
Not something we should hide.

But we must look at ourselves,
It all starts with us.
Thank yourself and your inner kid.
Your body is your home of love.
It's the only place where you truly live.
There is so much more to you.
So much more than you know you can give.
There are all the things you can't see.
All the broken bits and bobs and flaws and marks and odds and
sods that are a beautiful mystery.
Your scars tell a thousand stories.

Can I just start by saying how proud I am of you?
You have survived more things than I ever thought you could.
You have helped so many people along the way.
You have grown in so many ways.
Your darkness has given you wings.
Your strength has helped you to see better days.
And eyes to see the beauty in other things.
Your scars were beautiful lessons and badges of honour.
That helped you to heal and find ways to help and heal others.
Through all kinds of weather.
Even though you are getting older, you're becoming wiser with
every passing day.
You have come so far in painful shoes and never stopped along
the way.
To take them off or change your bloody socks.
You kept climbing every step, no matter how hard it got.
You have found your voice and your tribe
And your calling that yearns deep inside.
I am so glad to call you my best friend.
I'll be in your corner until the very end.

# YOU ARE ART

We were a jigsaw
With missing pieces
Trying to iron out all our problems
But we left too many creases
You are the oxygen
My lungs needed
The blood flow to my heart
Now depleted.
With you, life made sense
It was completed.
My demons,
Were silenced in your presence
You had them defeated.
You think you know how it will be
At the start
Love is the mystery we failed to solve
As we both fell apart
Your memories are an exhibition
Because every piece of you is art.

# PAPER HEART

Her heart was made of paper
So, it never bled
After all the harsh things
That were done and said.
She wanted an easy life
No creases
But she gave me plenty of paper cuts
She wanted a fresh sheet when enough was enough?

It was *love.*

That finally curled up her edges
Crushing her heart into a ball
Filling her with dread.
It was my tears that turned her heart
Into paper mâché instead.

# STAR CROSSED

Her heart exploded in front of me
Into thousands of tiny stars.
Like grains of salt in the sea.
Impossible to see by the human eye.
I tried to love every part of her but I was denied.
The secrets she buried so deeply inside.
Her pain and darkness she tried to hide.
Like it was a dead body.
The only thing she ever killed was my heart.
A cosmic kind of coronary.
She's gone now and her emptiness scares me.
But her soul lights up the sky at night.
It's the darkest thing
That makes her shine so bright.

# UNDER THE STARLIT SKY

This is where we all go
To run away or hide from our woes and sorrows.
Taking someone's hand
Under the stars
Our lips touch
The moon picks us out
Like a spotlight on stage
As we dance
Dance together under the starlit sky.
Friends drink and smoke
Play and joke.
Whilst we dance under the starlit sky.
This place is always busy
Except for when it rains
The collector of lost souls
Who missed their last trains
I found love that night.
Under the starlit sky.
Something far out of reach.
Always afraid, but in that moment I yield.
I lost my self and was reborn again
In those London fields.

# LOVE LIKE KRYPTONITE

I cannot be super
I cannot bend metal... yet.
I cannot be super
My red beam hasn't been checked.
Tell me your life in ten seconds.
Tell me you love me in two words.
Time isn't on your wrist or playing on your side.
Days are ticking away on a list of things you've never tried.

Fingertips we'll never touch it's hands too far out to reach.
Lessons we're not always prepared for
Students of life as she aims to teach.

Show me your secret powers.
While no-one is around.
I'm a hero of sorts.
Though not the kind you read about.
What do Superhero's do?

When they're not saving lives or fighting Super Villains.
Searching for love
To find that piece they're missing
In a sea of billions.

Your words deactivate my defences.
I can fly without my cape when you are near.
Your heart could light up cities for miles.
Your power is stronger than any of my fears.
Your beauty recharges the sun as she warms up the entire sky.

I'd take a thousand bullets for our kind of love.
As you watch a superhero bleed for real.
Then die.

# JUSTAGAME

Our souls chequered like a chessboard.
All the light and dark shades
We've had to fight our way through.
There was no black and white
It was acres of grey between me and you.
I took the **Queen** from you.
You killed the **King** in me.
So many pieces, sacrificed along the way.
Our love - was just a game.

The one neither of us knew how to play.

# BROKEN RECORD

Their truth wrapped up in a silk ribbon lie
That silver tongue moulded every word I see
Turned into art later hung up Infront of me
On the walls of my subconscious.
Your exhibition of pain like a soulless ghost train.
Limited addition, put inside an expensive frame.
Stealing away my money, as it rots away my brain.
I want to own your art a reminder of my role
The vinyl slung on the pin drops to play.
Scratched up like a chopping board.
Lyrics of love now in disarray.
Echo around the walls like a foreign language
Barely speak a word to each other, what can we say?
I stare in wonder at your masterpiece
Taken in by your talent and creative touch.
The devil is in the details the ones I didn't see.
Till it was too late open-heart surgery.
Scheduled for midnight.
As I wake up and see,
The gaping hole in my chest, this bloody mess.
Where our fairy-tale life used to be.

# FLOWERS IN A BROKEN POT

When we were together,
We were a book filled with a million stories.
Now we're coming to an end that was our time.
To think in your beautiful blank diary, I was the fine line.
We were the flowers in broken pots, decaying leaves among
mildew drops.
We're now an envelope of words that stopped.
As we are running out of things that can be said.
I'm sorry when you met me, I wasn't at my best.
Trapped deep inside my head.
Longing to find you in my heart.
But sadly, somethings were never said.
My gifts to you left scars and bruises.
Caught in a trap from previous abusers.
That's not me making up excuses.
You will grow daffodils, where I caused you pain.
Our ashes lye in the shadows of your new flame.
I'm glad you got out of my crippling maze.
I hope I find the exit myself one of these days.
Driving myself crazy like a parrot with clipped wings encaged.
Thinking to look in the mirror, but I'm too afraid.
Seeing you smile with a dancing heart,
Looking up watching stars with someone new.
Gives me hope in my future that someday I will too.

# LOVE TRIP

If love were a drug would we become addicts?
Once we get a taste of that sweet nectar.
It's impossible to deny it.
That feeling that makes us unstoppable.
Transported to that other world like a superhero.
Taking on the world protected by the powerful electric glow.
Giving you wings to take that high.
As you subconsciously prepare for the low.
The other half of us that may potentially go.
A comedown from love.
A pain that wrecks both heart and soul.
But when it's stolen away from us.
That special someone that was once in tow.
Ripped from that nourishing soil.
Feels impossible for anything good to grow.
A friend of mine was scared to fall in love.
Protected himself for years.
Denying himself joy held back by his multitude of fears.
To fall for someone that would shatter every piece of you if they
were gone.
We humans crave love, like flowers crave the sun.
To fall for someone from a skyscraper.
Is a pain that would kill like no other.
Many arrows from cupids bow missed and got stuck in the
wrong people.
But they didn't know.
And so, I have seen many couples stay together because it's
comfortable.

They are not the love interests sadly, they are just cameos.
If love lights fires and paints rainbows.
Sews up our pains but can create sorrows.
But love is hidden in amongst a sea of tomorrows.
So, don't give up on your search.
To find that missing piece,
Somewhere your love is upon this scorched Earth.

# WET PAINT

We were that painting left out in the storm.
Colourful drops of rain now fall.
Like a rainbow cried for us.
The grass is greener now, but for the wrong reasons.
Our beautiful ideas submerged into a colourful mess.
A kaleidoscope of chaos thrown together with what's left.
Canvas weaker now, wood soaked to breaking point.
An art attack by accident.
Modern art spilled across the ground.
An empty broken frame now.
A metaphor for us no longer being around.
The sun feels a shade darker now, the birds don't sing quiet as
loud.
Air feels less pure with you gone.
Our favourite song lacks its sweet sound.
Washed away in a storm.
Our love drops like acid rain,
Bringing colour to everything else.
As it leaves us both blank yet stained.

# TOXIC

The energy changes as I stain the room with our mood.
The pain eats up my happiness like left over food.
They can smell the fear I'm covered in
Suffocating as it snakes up my body leaving no room left for
oxygen.
Fangs full of poison getting ready to bite.
There's no antidote in sight.
Toxic blood floods my veins like chaos spreads through a train.
The house is burning but we're both to blame.
The fire was too much for our love to survive.
Romance wasn't sleeping, it had already died.
In our war there's no use picking sides.
We're a broken theme park with dangerous rides.
We can't break up God knows we've tried.
We pray for rain.
Millions of kisses to put out these flames.
But I'm the fire, you're the fuel,
I'm the joker, You're the fool.
Love isn't just a game, it's one of your many tools.
There's no cure for us. So, I watch it burn.
I broke your heart. Now it's your turn.

# BREAKING THE ICE

I prayed for rain; you gave me snow
The winter came killing that orange summers glow.
The cold winds thawed the lake we loved so
Reflecting the sky like we'd be walking on cloud nine.
Allowing me to walk on water as I quake.
The feeling I get asking you out.
The step I take wondering if I make the move?
To show you love but will the ice break.
As I fall into the depths. Freezing to death.
As the ice seals me in.
Never to see your face again.

# SILENT SOLITUDE

The silence of the rain stopped the birds singing in their tracks
Green light spilled across the graveyard from the traffic lights.
Memories of you I fight to get back.
In weather like this, we'd be kissing.
It's the smell of you this world is missing.
I try not to notice the black void of space where you once were.
My hair, clothes and skin soaked to the bone.
Trying to take this all in.
If I cried now would you hear me?
From way up there in the blue.
Wasted tears now fall, decapitated words leave me speechless.
I never said I loved you.

# WHERE DOES THE TRUTH LIE?

How much pain?
Will remain from a white lie?
When you kill the truth.
Do you use a bullet or will bare hands do?
As your victims watch on, and perhaps they are guilty of the
same thing as you.
Picking up bits of broken reality searching for all the clues.
Who is better with the lie? Me or you?
As I feel my open wounds cry.
I understand or at least I try.
The stitches punching out through my skin.
All that painful waterfall of sin
Blood sealed up like a letter under the skin.
As you try to catch the tears I cried.
A souvenir in your rusty heart shaped tin.
But your lies have stained my insides.
Black or white? I'll let you decide.
A lie is a lie.
As we try to cross this chessboard where truth is crucified and
left to die.
Were you ever friends with the truth? I'll let you decide.
Your words cut like a knife.
I'm left shaken,
My world reshaped by your lie.
I'm that worthless jigsaw now with missing pieces and a broken
sky.
Lies are fake hope, I hope you realise.
There is even Lies in realise if you put the E Infront of the I.
Crazy right?

Your hope is a fake friend or foe.
A hornet's nest gift wrapped neatly with a golden bow.
A ticking time bomb of truth that will one day blow.
I'm denying you the best parts of me, I know.
The God's honest truth.
That I abuse,
Let loose on a flower, you pull every petal off and hand me the
stem.
Because you love the power.
A pick and mix of the story that I choose to digest slowly, Hour
after hour.
Like a fly pukes on its food to consume.
I think on our conversation I'm confused by the lack of truth.
You think your winning this as I lose
But you're only lying to yourself that's the ironic truth.
Your lies were dreams without the monster at the end.
Your lies where something wild.
A world you built around us that was a poisonous pretend.
You took my eyes with your lies
Removed my smile with every mile upon mile.
Your imagination ran away with you.
Leaving me behind without a clue.
You cut me a thousand times as I lay in burgundy sheets.
Your side of the bed is cold
Whenever I think of our time together.
My heart skips a beat.
I would scour the earth without shoes looking for you that's the
truth.
As I count all the blisters on my bloody feet.
You win. But what a luscious defeat.

# IT'S JUST WORDS

It's just words,
That's all we ever had,
Whether it was texts on screen,
Or words I didn't know how to express left on a note pad.
It's just words we said to each other across a table,
A moment that now haunts my mind.
As I want to go back, rewind so I can relive those sublime times
we shared.
Before I cared, too much.
Maybe that's what made you scared.
But it's just words.
Now it's words on a screen, quickly deleted, ones that'll never
be seen.
You were the one from my recurring dreams.
A ghost my mind must have made up.
As you disappeared from my world, or so it seems.
I feel like I'm going behind your back with your answer phone.
She's the only version of you that's ever home.
Just hearing your voice helps for some reason when I'm on my
own.
My words used to break a smile,
I haven't seen your kind of happiness in a while.
We used to share words with each other every day.
Now I look at a blue screen with an empty display.
My mind now filled with a field of words I don't know how to
say.
Unable to form sentences for you now.
Whereas it was easy when it was a two-way.
I watched your beautiful long messages slowly shrink away.

As you ran out of things to say.
Until all your ink had faded and the colours now gone.
As I'm left jaded.
Leaving my world ice cold and grey.
Like granite,
Everything was amazing just how we'd planned it.
Now it's like we're living on different planets.
And to tell you the truth I can't handle it.
I wrote a song about you, it's all I could do.
Lyrics when I tasted a glimpse of the future, that's no longer true.
Because it doesn't involve just us two.
I think of all the words you'd say to the new person in your life.
I envy their ears and eyes.
That soak up your words, as I read over your old ones and cry.
It's the lack of your sentences that hurt.
Was I in love with you or your lovely words?
I revisit our conversation, a souvenir of our time together.
Archived away in a secret location.
Sometimes you don't get the person you truly adore.
It was the kind of world I wished for, forever tangled up in your words.
And by your side.
So many sentences that died, from far too many times from drunken tries.
All the love I have for you I now sadly must hide.
Burning up this field of words that ache for you.
That's buried deep inside.
You used to finish my sentences, now there's no more replies.
We were a rebound in disguise.
Once the real thing,
Now we're just words.
Lyrics from my song that I yearn to sing.

# FALLING FOR A PHOTO

I've written to the edge of every page,
From caves filled from our hidden pains,
Where the memories of you continue to stain,
Every frame of my life.
Like fingerprints on polaroid's my heart was your plaything,
Until you broke that toy.
You'd play the field as the nocturnal vampire came out.
Out there sucking pleasure from the others you seek
In secret locations or dark alley ways where you'd creep.
I was the fool on the edge of love that fell too deep.
Worried sick and losing sleep.
As you strip me bare, taking your pounds of flesh,
With plenty of interest.
Eyes on you like a spotlight so many drawn into your gaze,
Like sex crazed moths that wanted to misbehave.
They could smell the excitement off you for miles.
Your natural scent drew them in.
Like blood hounds they'd gather around the tables.
I thought that you were an angel, an angel that was addicted to
sins,
As I'm forced to fight with no chance to win.
Not knowing what's wrong or right.
Arguments on repeat the track that played for us each night.
Haunted by your sweet songs, red lipstick, and black thongs.
But where did it all go wrong?
"Black velvet and that little boy's smile"
These lyrics clawed their way into my mind as they haunt me
still for miles.
Trust was that bridge between us that cracked and fell apart.

Eaten away by every time you betrayed me.
I can count the tally marks across my heart.
Every time that knife went in your dark version came out.
Your dual personality, trying to love the two of you but I had my doubts.
Falling for a photo hanging on the wall.
My mind lost in a maze of love as you caved in all those walls,
And watch me free fall.
Tears for my last performance as we hear the crowd applaud.
I'm broken hearted. I'm that tear-soaked shirt crumpled on the floor.
How many times can you try to fix the glass in a stain glass window?
When that piece doesn't seem to fit anymore.
Knowing every time, the sun glows, the cracks will always show.
And one day when the wind is too strong, that fragment of glass will eventually go.
A kaleidoscope of a love I hoped would work.
But those broken pieces were the lessons we needed to find better hearts.
As ours were far too damaged from the start.
Don't fall for a photo on a wall.
Loving someone you've never met at all.
As your mind creates a perfect story, one that couldn't exist.
Haunted by that happy ending, even when it goes a miss.
It's my fault. My hopes were too high.
As I put you way up there on a pedestal.
As I watched our fairy tale love take a fatal fall.

# POEMS
# ABOUT
# PAIN

# DON'T HIDE YOUR PAINS INSIDE

Four walls black as sin
A soul on the edge struggles within,
The truth trapped inside like paint dries as the darkness slowly
sets in.
This is where the nightmares begin.
We see the cries for help, across their skin.
But do we jump in?
Do we take the time to do what's right?
Or do we leave them alone to fight that fight.
Invisible wars are doing more damage than we can ever know,
How many wrongs till we do what's right?
That's just the way it goes cold bodies on slabs.
Labels now on their wrists and ankles as they longer use their
big toes.
Demons we bear in mind tally up their scores.
As the body count soars from so many souls that are sore.
Why are so many lives taken so often?
What is all this killing for?
They tried as we cried.
Scars on their flesh, as their demons subside.
But let's not be blind.
This is happening all the time.
Too many souls taken in the blink of an eye.
Tell me why?
Why is darkness so heavy to hold?
Too difficult to tell another living soul.
An impossible load, too much pain to behold.
Searching for answers in a dark room, like pirates search for
gold.

But this isn't something new. This is old.
People taking their lives and leaving a warm bed cold.
I've known people drowning in their dark.
Looking for any kind of light,
A matchstick flick to create some hope even a spark.
But It's just the start.
Words are their weapons against the dark.
But it's hard when fear sews their lips tight.
Looking for the right words to tell someone your pain is the real fight.
Suicide is a decision that the hurting decide.
But we need those people to pick a different side to suicide.
To tighten the seat strap on their roller coaster ride.
So, that they can survive.
People who have been on the edge,
With nothing left, Yet they saved themselves,
Coming back from off the ledge.
An inspiring role model to speak the truth that was never said.
The demons win when we stay silent.
Speak your pain and truth and disarm the Tyrant.
Too much time is spent, entrapped in emotional cement.
Concrete problems or so it seems.
But those foundations can be broken and in those cracks grow positive seeds.
A nightmare dies as life blossoms into beautiful dreams.
A life that seemed out of reach.
Is now in your hands, as you found your way.
And now your words can inspire and teach.
Reaching out to those lost in the dark sea
Drowning in the deep end of their misery.
As they make that important discovery
A chain breaker that can tell others, how to break free.
And live a life full of wonder entranced by mother nature's flawless beauty.

# CELL YOURSELF

That's time!
As the bell rings.
The remnants of that double vodka still stings,
As I think over things.
Last orders at the bar,
But I was always a bit of gambler,
Going back home to my family sober was irregular.
I'd end up on the street or in the gutter.
I was always pushing things to far,
Tempting fate with my near misses using up all my hallelujahs.
This time I hear another bell, one that's much closer now.
The one echoing next to the wall of my cell.
I've got a one to one with the devil,
He's booked me front row seats in hell.
This time I'm doing here, all the Beatings I take.
From the others who've sinned.
A cursed life now, from their one mistake.
Hoping to catch a break from the ghosts of the souls.
They were too quick to take.
Praying for forgiveness for goodness' sake.
It's just four years that's all it will take.
But it keeps taking and taking,
My mind is on the edge, cracks on the surface, close to breaking,
Wearing a smile for the screws in this place is draining.
Pain staking phone calls from broken families.
Photos of people we can no longer see,
A funeral is the closest thing to a holiday.
That's what they say but it feels like I'm serving life.
It is a life sentence for taking a life for my lack of sense.

When I leave this prison and return home haunted by the reason.
That guilt haunts my mind and soul.
As I fight my demons to gain control, holding strong, but I think they know.
While all the while, steps Infront for my future,
Feels like walking the green mile.
I never would have imagined this as my life
When I was that cheeky angelic child.
But how life is a roller-coaster for those on the edge born to be wild.

As I while away my days too afraid to face myself
Or visit their grave.
A soul I took that can't be saved.
I walk around like a ghost now too afraid to embrace my days.
Thinking of ways to tell them how sorry I am.
Repent for the demons that made me that kind of man.
Learn to embrace that was who I am.
But I need to lead a good life for the one that now stains my hands.
That life I took isn't gone.
They're the vision in everything I see,
I hope one day their family can find the strength to forgive me.

# THE WARS IN WARRIORS

I've spent too long living inside the ruins of bad days.
Afraid to trust in my dreams as they dissipate.
Demon's dance across my mind like it's a chess board
Hungry for their check mate.
As those harsh thoughts breach the gate.
Pawns that storm the kingdom to take the king down.
Watching royalty weakened as bent knees quake
The crown falls as war will break.
A dark passenger planting toxic seeds.
Weaved deep into the fabric of me.
The mirror with a thousand faces, so my reflection isn't seen.
The emptiness that fills these days.
Trapped with those thoughts in a rusting cage.
I've won every battle on that bloody stage
And even though I'm a warrior…

I'm still afraid.

# BETTER WAYS

Rain falls,
Like thoughts fail,
The harsher they hit turning into hail.
Our mind like a Scalextric track,
Round and round,
Poisoning thoughts impossible to retract.
Dizzying dystopian drips fall into my day terror trips.
Forget the nightmares there's no medicine for this kind of sick.
We're like all those ships caught in the storm.
A slow release of venom lying dormant, since the day we were born.
We were forewarned that life is no picnic.
You must battle with or without it.
Pretending to be blind so, we have an excuse for missing all the signs.
Get on top of our mental maze, where the aftermath can scar for days.
But when the storm clears we can see there are better ways.

# SPLIT

Pain, you have always been the author of my life
But it's time for this story to end.
You have been a great teacher but sadly a terrible friend.
I love the parts of me you have tormented
They have had most of my time.
You've stolen many moments from me but always kept me in
line.
The next chapters we have, we shall deal with alone.
You live your life now. I'll live my own.

# WOUNDS IN WONDERLAND.

The storm approaching
As, my curtains dance.
I twist and recoil.
A magpie's call, breaks me from my trance.

Numb to it all I begin to fall.
Her scent hits me
As I begin to recall.

Suffocate my wrist.
One last trip to Disneyland
On, the VIP list.
That sharp pain,
Shoots straight into my vein
The mosquito of my dreams with its deadly aim.

The darkness creeps in.
As my mind transforms.
Like a shape shifter.
Between these four walls.

It splits in two like Siamese twins.
Ripping at the seams
Her lying there, breathless.
In and out of these lucid dreams.
My wounds start pulsating.
Scars like dot to dot,
Along my ankles and wrists,
I love her sweet whispers,

But fear her fatal kiss.
Like the poisonous apple.
I fall in love after just one bite.

I prefer something far wilder.
That craving calls me into the night,
As the rage fuels my blood.
Breaking out of this cage
My thirst far beyond,
This battered up place.

I must leave her now
For one last taste.
As the calm wind howls.
She takes me by the hand.
Guiding me off swiftly,
To get lost in Wonderland.

# WORRY

I'm hiding between each thought
Like concrete between bricks.
Worrying you like mad.
Worrying you sick.
I'm there to greet you in the morning.
Or wake you from a peaceful sleep.
I'm connected to so many things.
Diluting your happiness like a wolf ravishes the sheep.
I'll go for now but be back soon.
I'm not sure if you noticed but I enjoy tormenting you.

# INVISIBLE WALLS

You creep up around me when I'm not looking
You try to steal my day but I'm starting to see your game plan.
You've given yourself away.
As the world became more distorted
Like mud finds itself in a puddle
You've been messing with my mind and body so long.
Turning my life into a puzzle.
You have affected too many people and now we have an army.
We will deal with you once and for all Anxiety.
As we unleash a mindfulness tsunami.

# STRING ME ALONG

I breathe life into you
As your red rubber skin expands.
Into a strange shape
My lungs like a flexible cage
Slowly start to ache.
I hope you'll float with me for days.
But I'm scared with me, you won't be safe
You keep my mind and spirits up.
Have I invested in you too much faith?
Can you save me from drowning?
Taking all the weight and worries of this world.
I can imagine your face now frowning.
As everything hangs on by a string.
Elevate me from this pain I bare.
That haunts me every day.
Carry me from the depths of despair.
As we glide far far away.
You slip through my hands like a knife, whisked away in a gust.
I forgive you for letting me down.
I was a fool to give you all my trust.
You could never save me that way.
You are just a balloon
It was me that got carried away.

# ENEMY INSIDE

Don't respond well to responsibility
It disables me.
If my opportunities were all balloons,
Then anxiety is the enemy.
Deflating happiness with its sharp wit
Every last pin prick is a hard hit,
You sunk my battleship!
But I'm not sick.
Not satisfied till it's drank up my life,
Every last f**king sip.
I want it to let go,
As I finally get a grip.
I can't allow my mind to be hijacked
Taking me for joyrides along train tracks.
This is my life, it's time to claw my way back.
Haven't figured out the art of how to relax
People cheat their way there with Prozac.
Running from your shadow's a waste of time.
Were you hidden in my childhood?
Did I imagine everything was just fine?
You're the scariest demon I must face,
There's an exorcism about to take place.
My mind like a house of mirrors creating the worst-case
scenario.
Once a *Novice* at fighting your darkness long ago.
Better watch out because now I'm a **Pro**.

# FLOSSING WITH HEART STRINGS

Toxic coated lips like a kiss from poison Ivy.
Bone dry conversations syllables stolen like Elephants tusks sold
for ivory.
You think you can read my mind well just try me.
It's only a cardboard cut-out or digital perception that you can
see.
I'm those static flickers of code dancing through your TV.
I tried to share my life like a three-course meal, but you got too
greedy.
We talk about love being dangerous if you fall from high up.
And you fell far too easy.
We have so many fights trying to find a way to agree.
You fill my mind with junk as those thoughts are far too filthy.
My heart stopped like broken clocks from your sheer beauty.
I have a darkness like a wild animal that is far too beastly.
We always had that poor mindset
Notes would fly by as we counted every penny.
You think you know who I am?
But it's time to wake up and smell the coffee.
We force fed this house too much furniture as both our hearts
we're so empty.
You tattooed my skull with harsh thoughts like they were
graffiti.
You gain satisfaction by soaking up all the misery.
Your complex thoughts are the swings and roundabouts that
leave my world dizzy.
Trying to find common-sense in your sentences is far too hazy.
We're two sides of a dangers coin lodged inside one brain but
that's just a theory.

I'm that mist that appears when someone rubs you up the wrong way
Like I'm some kind, of twisted genie.
You can cut me out of the pictures but I'm going nowhere.
Because I've stained your memory.
We are each other's invisible scars
That turn to damaged art upon our hearts that struggle to restart.
As we tear them apart like Lions do to zebras in wild Safari Parks.
You are the bear that roams around the forest inside my mind.
We bring darkness to each other's lives like we removed each other's eyes.
The wrong love is like a cluster bomb a mind f**k filled with a nasty surprise.
Was it lust that left us both blind?
Flicking through happy memories like polaroid's or were they just lies?
We devoured each other's hearts like drunk cannibals that hadn't even realised.

# FOR SHADOWS

The Shadows aren't just behind me in the light.
They cling to me in the dark.
Listening to the rhythm like a beating drum, from my
overactive heart.
Whispering tales of misfortune trying to paint my future.
Into a painfully colourful picture.
Abusing the truth as it sews it up into a thinly veiled sheet.
So neatly made just to cover my eyes.
These shadows stalk my every move now.
As if my soul was the prize.
Hidden in cracks in doorways or random objects I pass by.
Shadows waiting at the bottom of the stairs,
Not even God knows why.
Shadows that follow me home
Shadows of the weak and broken that are now walking alone.
Hordes of them come to see me sulking around corners.
As they've lost the bodies they used to own.
I'm a magnet for fallen shadows but I wish they wouldn't live in
my head.
They're all filled with a thousand stories of sad tales that were
never said.

# PAINFUL REMINDER

If my pain bank was made from money instead.
I'd be a millionaire,
And with all the wealth I own all that pain wouldn't compare.
I could buy the best medical care.
But this bank is just a volt of pain that's going nowhere.
I wish a heist could steal it away.
I know they say,
That pain is a beautiful reminder, reminding you you're alive
each day.
But when it takes over your body from the inside you just want
to run and hide.
Pain is having a wail of a time deep inside my aching bones and
shaking mind.
Like it's having some kind of rave or wild party without me.
My body looking like a crack den.
As I return to my pen and ideas once again.
As I make myself dizzy with ways to appease my dis-ease.
Sad to be sad and wearing fake smiles constantly.
But what happens when the smiles run out?
Do I laugh, scream run or shout?
Lose my mind and my where abouts.
Head spinning from this pain like I'm stuck doing doughnuts in
a car around a roundabout.
Because I'm driven by pain.
Maybe there is a way to break free.
That doesn't involve ending my life and there for ending me.
After I count to three.

One
Two
Three...
Maybe I should just breath and take it easy.
Every day is different for me,
You see something I want you to see.
Beyond my flesh is a tomb of encased misery.
My mind plagued by jealousy,
For all the other humans that I see.
Pain has clipped its leash firmly around me,
Taking me for walks around the city,
Every day is a wishing list,
For these aches and imbalances to go a miss,
Or be dismissed.
But that's ridiculous because it's just a wish.
Like blowing candles out on a cake.
In my dreams I walk the streets with ease.
Living a life like all of you, make no mistake.
But when I wake, I sadly realise it's not true.
Pulled back down to reality like super glue.
Haunted by all those sentences of those professionals that
couldn't help me.
Chronic pain isn't a sentence sadly, for some it's a reality.
This canvas of life right in front of me,
I spit, flick blood at it, and cover it with mud as I scream.
I wish all this pain that surrounds my being,
Was nothing but a horrible dream.

# ONE PUSH

No one can see what goes on, on the inside.
Behind the dark windows there lies a woman with black eyes.
And a broken soul.
Beaten black and blue, a souvenir from her love.
The man she never really knew.
But as people pass by their house, they wouldn't have a clue.
On the inside It's cosy and warm for a few,
It's okay for some they keep us safe where others bring harm.
In nine months, I leave, hard to believe.
We never saw that side to Steve.
How can anyone raise a hand to a woman?
When we're supposed to live in unison.
No man would walk this earth if it wasn't for them.
One push, heart pounding
Sweat pouring, pain soaring
One push taken too far that morning.
As she went flying back
His way of dealing with things that he lacks.
As his darkness attacks.
"One more push", the doctor says,
You'll need to leave that house It's not a warning, It's a harsh
fact.
Her inner voice crying out,
Leave now while your mind and body are still intact.
One push we can almost see the beauty of life.
One push as she falls against the floor.
Her body broken, eyes red and swollen
Heart stolen, mind fucked

Time that wasted,
The time he sucked from her. How did a dream life?
Melt into a nightmare.
She was beauty, he was the beast.
She tried to see the good intentions deep within.
Tried to leave, but never made it a reality.
Drowning in a million dark violent hands,
That she struggled to understand lying there on the ground.
Her last thoughts spinning around,
The eerie silence
A high pitch breaks through the muffled TV sound.
No more screaming, no more hits.
No more taking any more of his shit.
That was the last push she'll ever take.
That was the last push he'll ever give her.
Trying to save him was her final mistake.
A love that tears you up like being hugged by barbwire.
They got on like a house on fire.
Till she suffocated in all the smoke.
A happy ending was a sick joke.
Her blood stains the rustic coffee table.
Furniture they bought when they were in love when he was
much kinder and more stable.
She couldn't save him, she wore his many bruises like satin.
Caught in his mind maze she was his plaything as he
misbehaved.
Too many hits, like an album from past dates.
He knocked her off her feet but not in the right way.
The knocks, cutting deep like razor blades.
Tarnished fairy tales from too many close shaves,
His last violent act, like ripping waves.
His final attack she was an innocent woman, yet he didn't hold
back.
One more push was how she leaves this world.
One more push, congratulations the doctor yells, "It's a girl."

# IN MY BLOOD

You're all too easy for me to deceive
I lie, like you breathe
Its claws are in deep.
I'm drowning out here as land is too far to reach.
Don't need money I'll use my charm.
This addiction is my pain so there's no need to self-harm.
Pockets empty since day one
Veins full of weeks gone
Escape artist on the run
I'm like the invisible man perfecting my magic tricks.
Doctors test what they can't fix.
Hyper now haven't even started on the Weetabix.
I've pulled the wool over so many still.
Too far gone, I'm over the hill.
I'm way beyond pills.
This thing sucks like a leech that's out to kill.
Take, take, take...as the stakes rise.
Some days I feel paralysed, other days just fly bye.
I'm duped by this fake paradise.
Head crushed inside this vice.
Don't give me the chance to lie.
Creating alibis by the wayside walls I've built to protect my
damaged pride.
What's next? Some new drug that I haven't tried.
I laugh as *they cry*.
You feel *the lows*, as I hit my highs.
If you could see how I've become blind,
Phantom images through red raw eyes,
Life's a dangerous game now as I roll the dice.

# FRAGILE BIRDS

Dear Anxiety,
Why did you choose me?
Am I special?
Or was I just easy.
Anxiety is the pandemic you won't see on TV.
There's no face mask that protects from this little doozy.
I'd say let's go our separate ways.
But truth be told, you help with these poems.
That fill the page diluting my rage.
Breaking me free if only for a moment from your claustrophobic cage.
The one I've been a tenant in for far too many days.

# BEAUTIFULLY BROKEN

You said you lacked emotions heartless now and left broken.
Loves damaging wounds exposed and raw in the open.
And you didn't believe that I could mend them.
Did my love heal some of those wounds?
Enough to make you feel loved in every room.
But it was an emotion you never really knew.
My love was drowning, and I was the waves crashing down on you.
But wouldn't a drought leave you more confused?
I want you to see the parts of me you mistook.
The version of me you broke, to fit into your look.
The foundation of me, that you had me shook.
Photo scraps of different types of love scattered across pages that form an unreadable book.
But now I see there were parts of me in amongst those broken nooks.
Chipped away and shapes that changed overtime, like statues with missing features now unrecognisable as they lie.
The scars I now wear from your many sins,
I want you to lose, like I lose when you win.
I want you to hurt, like you hurt me to death.
I guess it's safe to say I still have some of that past rage left.
But these are moments unsaid that I had to remove from my chest.
I want you to see how life is when you question past regrets.
I want you to know how hard it is to talk when crying takes away every breath.
I want you to walk down that road where my knuckles bled.
From anger and the rage of a complex love that was encaged.

But maybe it was me, that you were trying to save?
From the darkness coursing through your veins.
As I was willing to capsize and go down with the ship, it's true.
A darkness that would have torn us in two.
Too many pieces to try to piece back together and sadly you knew.
We'd have to pick up what's left.
But I truly understand now that you were actually at your best.
Thinking of a way to save me from your dark mess.
We never got to say goodbye.
Our ending was digital heart break by text.
Because your last words were unspoken.
Fractured happy memories of us still haunt me.
As I'm left beautifully broken.

# BALANCING ACT

My life of late,
Has been a balancing act, crossing that tightrope whilst juggling plates.
It feels like I'm falling without a safety net.
No ambulance on standby for a pulse to check.
Feeling like you're constantly on a boat at sea.
Without ever touching the water.
Like you've been cursed by a witch.
Some kind of Voodoo or a new kind of torture.
Jealous of people for having a normal life.
But what does normal mean?
In this grand scheme of things?
Feeling Like Icarus falling with broken wings.
To stand on both feet again, feeling the earth under me.
To be rooted deep in the ground like a wise old tree.
Who is it that takes, my balance from me?
I've sailed through storms so easily.
Why is normal the hardest thing.
Like a child learning to walk.
To be balanced, would make my heart sing.

# IS IT DARK ENOUGH?

Is it dark enough yet?
When pain's the only thing that stays.
As it rains for days thinking of better ways to pass the time.
But the guilt has already set.
Like a concrete problem in the mind that you can't forget.
Is it dark enough yet?
When money is drawn to those in high-rise apartments,
Living life carefree
No money concerns and a distinct lack of arguments.
Whereas those beneath on the streets
Barely any food in their bellies or shoes on their feet.
A bizarre contrasting reality,
Some enjoying the fruits of life other's confused by humanity.
Is it dark enough yet?
When class divides crash together like trains do in train sets.
Envy those with better clothes, better health,
More awards and medals on their shelves.
As they had the guts to push themselves.
Is it dark enough yet?
That if we were gone would people miss us?
Tell tales about us.
Live in lyrics of their songs?
Will they carry parts of us in their hearts or have I got it wrong?
Is it dark enough yet?
When words no longer mean a thing
Birds no longer continue to sing
Nature silenced; we don't hear anything.
Is there a glimmer of hope we can bring?
Is it dark enough yet?

When the sun no longer sets, when the moon forgets.
And the stars have nothing left to reflect.
A darkness, that's impossible to forget.
Red fills the sea for miles, ice has cracked over a thousand smiles.
As the world becomes far too wild.
Is it dark enough yet?

# BACK ACHE

Yes, we hear this a lot.
I apologies, but sadly its true.
I think we should pin the blame on chairs.
That's where I stand. How about you?

I got myself in debt trying to fix it.
It felt like an impossible task.
I've tried Osteopaths, physios' and acupuncture,
But nothing seems to last.

It's like the pain doesn't want to leave you.
Cosy inside like a pet.
I tell you this for nothing.
Those bills rack up just the same, as if you were seen by the vet.

# LIE LIKE A LULLABY

Once upon a time I kissed your lies a thousand times.
My lips eroded before my eyes
Words from your tongue were demonized.
Stealthily Stealing away vital organs, before I realised.
Toxic love is dangerous, that shouldn't come as a surprise.
My Teeth fall out and break like China plates.
Mistakes we made to order, pain delivered to our door like
takeaways.
Holding hate inside, buried deep like an emotional grenade.
As my heart explodes, my blood-stained mess comes out to play.
One last time, I beg you to stay.
Before the silence between us ebbs away,
Our relationship on life support as we watch it slowly die.
Make my ears bleed, as your lips divide.
One last taste as I digest your final lie.

# BE MY GUEST

Like me, hype me.
Set fire to me and watch me burn.
Falling into holes as you laugh, I learn.
You show a true side behind your smile and charming eyes.
There is more to you besides.
You see talent like butterflies.
You want to catch in glass jars so that you can spy.
A private performance where the talent is trapped inside.
But will that satisfy?
What happens when they can no longer fly?
Their colours fade as you watch them slowly die.
Plucking them straight out of the sky.
You couldn't help yourself, you just had to try.
When their wings are broken and tattered,
And their distinct colourful patterns no longer matter
Like broken art frames, where crowds no longer gather.
Genuine on the surface,
Your skin like a mask you wear.
But you revealed too many clues
Your truth you thought was hidden but I could see right
through.
All the layers of lies, friendship was something we both gave a
try.

But between you and I,
This friendship was bound to fail, as there were hidden holes in
the sails.
There was something wrong something lacked.
Because I prefer real people that are kind and helpful and have
your back.

If you trip and stumble not laughing with the crowd
As they take a bow and we take a tumble.
Was this your show after all?
I was just a guest who, you tried to make a fool?
Trapped in your ego nest.
Behind charm and charisma was your damaging tool.
You'd strip away parts of us and keep your cool.
Like picking wings off butterflies,
As they struggle to take off, you'd watch on with pride.
Be careful of certain friend requests they can be a can of worms
in disguise.

The bait used to get you hooked.
But once they pull you out of the sea you suddenly find it
impossible to breathe.
Like a fish out of water take it from me.
They'll watch you at your worst wearing a smile.
But be absent at your best.
I guess our friendship wasn't legit, it was just another test.
Can we still be friends? *No*, I'd reply.
But you can always *be my guest*.

# DARK FOREST

Trauma in our lives,
Are like a cave of vampires feeding off our insides,
We need to bring them into the light.
Watch them explode into a cloud of dust and blown out of sight.
We've become friends with our darkness and strangers to the light.
Letting go of that heavy pain as we slowly trust in ourselves once again.
Images of aching memories on constant play back,
A merry-go-round of moments that left a dent or crack.
Our memories go round. Stuck on repeat.
Following the same denial track nothing merry about that.
Except a chance now to change our tact.
Frightened to trust in uplifting colours again as too many people painted my world black.
Feelings that felt wrong.
Buried inside a straitjacket singing my favourite song.
Demons I've brought to the surface in the sea of truth.
Not an easy place for one to swim through.
Where haunting memories float insight.
Truth hurts more than pain eating away at us through the night.
Tentacles of complex emotions built into our minds like a computer game.
We have to find a way to give our darkness a name.
Being brave to drag them up onto the shore.
Unsure of why we never did this before.
Where darkness drinks from our innocent well of youth.
Drunk on the blood from our stale truth.

A truth we can no longer ignore.
We all have skeletons in our closets,
But what are we hiding behind that locked door?
Bring truth to the light,
As dark crippling hands that were once too tight.
Slowly release their grip.
A séance of hope for one's future spirit.
Leaving behind a damaged trip.
Our trauma removed from us like a decaying tooth.
Out of our own dark forest of thoughts, safely swept away in a stream of truth.

# DISMANTLED SOUL

Would our pains meet in the plains amongst fields of hope?
Understanding one another
Being able to be each other's lifeboat.
Pain is the language we are both fluent in.
Is that the place where healing begins?
Is pain Karma from our many sins we made by accident?
Cracks in our souls filled with weak cement.
Concrete thoughts created foundations of solitude
That kidnapped our children of youth.
Force feeding them lessons of a painful truth.
A conveyer belt of constant abuse, as hope is drained of its
essential juice.
The acid pools we all swam through,
Searching for clues to piece together what makes you, you.
Stained flesh, charged skin, bones on display, nothing hidden.
We are transparent for the world to see.
The dolls in the shop window of pain and misery, that can't be
set free.
The pen is our sword as well as our therapy.
I swear there is a lesson somewhere,
Amongst these wounds and confused traumatised bruised rooms
we bare,
Where no visitors would ever choose to rest a while.
They wouldn't dare.
These walls ache by the very same pains we had to take.
Hanging up picture's frames over the cracked walls,
Like fake smiles for the crowds to swallow.
So, we have been framed.
Taking the blame for the pain we struggle to explain.

We allowed them to play a character in our mind game.
Hidden in plain sight, yet we feel the shame in the silent night.
Tears that run into the dark corners of our lonely room.
Where voices plague our minds through thin walls
As we turn crazy like the looney tunes.
We played the crowd so well but poets' words are their true tell.
A tale that tells the pain they prevailed.
Sailed the harsh storms with every stanza
Written with their own blood as their hands are aching,
Over translating pieces of their dismantled souls,
Lessons littered with nuggets of gold.
Taking a stand against the demon's plan
To sabotage a future that's in our hands.
We stay and fight, whilst others ran.
But I can understand it's not easy
When our fights are invisible to so many.
Battling demonic clowns that aren't around in other people's
sights.
They're not haunted by their sounds, keeping us awake at night.
That jingle bell, the encore of a hell, that's making so many
souls unwell.
And we don't have the words or strength to tell.
As they make us the fool as we try to yell, inside our box with a
million locks.
Screaming at the top of our voices but those words are lost.
Empathetic tentacles wrap round our open wounds,
As we taste each other's pains, it's the blood we consume.
And gain strength for our next fight.
Like a vampire gains power from the blood of another.
We too are cursed with certain insights.
Making a home out of our darkness but taunted by the light.

# BOX OF PAIN

Bravery isn't bloody battle fields with crimson coated blades and aching bones.
It's helping those, who are battling darkness alone?
Lips gripped and sealed with fear.
Frozen to the spot like a rabbit in headlights, or a traumatised dear.
Smiles drawn on as their happiness, slowly disappears.
What happens when they run out of smiles?
Does the real them reappear?
Will we understand their pain?
As they speak in the language of tears.
Sparing others from their dark box of pain, afraid to open the lid once again.
Crushed by the weight of their guilt and shame.
But they are not the ones to blame.
That's all part of darkness's cruel game.
Scared to let anybody in.
Sharing your darkness with someone else isn't a sin.
Speak through those dark walls so your demons don't win.
It's not an easy journey but it's one that must begin.
Darkness isolating the vulnerable like a pack of lions' hunt to kill.
Their four walls getting tighter still.
Mistakenly, thinking they'd leave others happy,
If their absence was present, instead of themselves.
As they are hell bent on thinking they need make amends.
For the dark maze they find themselves in.
As they take yet another pill
A prescription reminding them they are mentally ill.

Hurting themselves to feel if they still feel,
Their world transformed into a nightmare no longer knowing what's real.
We don't know the storm they're in, hidden behind that sunny painting.
As they fight inside their own skin.
Feeling like an empty shell
A space filled like an echoing chamber of hell.
Voices in your head constantly telling you you're not well.
Stealing away our words, so it's impossible to tell.
Words are weapons against the dark arts like a magic spell.
That inner storm that pulls lives apart,
But we can all make a start.
Having these heart to hearts.
We don't have the answers to their problem,
But we can just be two ears to listen.
Or two arms to hold them.
As they find their feet and hope once again,
But before it comes to their suicide,
We can take their side,
Before their split in the middle and forced to decide.
Or be in their lane,
A key to the light is giving our darkness a name.
Tears are strength, bravery is truth
When their lives are caved in we can be their roof.
Be that kind in humankind that's a kind of proof.
Show them a place of kindness that we can all create.
Because in real life Superhero's don't wear capes.

# BACK TO FRONT

It's no wonder people get jacked up.
Turning to alcohol they get, tanked up.
Fighting a drug habit, smacked up.
Drown this pain with that buzz just to shut it up.
Pain is the puppeteer master keeping me suspended in mid-air.
So badly want to touch the ground but I'm getting nowhere.
Looking for sympathy it doesn't care.
Wake up.
Spine like a deck of cards out of whack.
Hit the yoga mat.
Twisting like a coil
Trying to find a way to stand.
It's hard being broken, when on the outside everything looks grand.
So, people can't truly understand.
Like one of pains malicious plans.
It's like some sick, magic trick.
Taking away my balance, just for kicks.
The pain like a train has been derailed.
Falling from a cliff just to be impaled on those harsh rocks of reality.
My mind shipwrecked like a boat at sea.
Pecked to death by seagulls.
People think they have the answer 'Mr Know It All'.
Like I broke all the rules.
Made a deal with the devil in the light house.
He gets to take over my life now.
I'm left with the Joker in my hand.
Drowning at sea but suffocating on land.

Envy of people that can walk with ease.
Riding storms searching for that inner peace.
Just to be pain free.
The tears I'd cry would drown an entire city.
Left diluting these pains through a rhyme.
Time to take my life back.
Back life my take to time.

# POEMS
# ABOUT
# POETRY

# MY LIFE IN PIECES

There were times among those bleeding rhymes where I was dissatisfied.
From free-flowing ideas and memories that never took flight.
They had crashed and died.
Killed one at a time, like an abortion they were murdered inside.
From that sharp swinging pendulum of judgement
Like the executioner's axe, maybe we could never have been artists,
If our hearts and souls were never attacked.
A tact we create like a well written play on stage
Where the crowds come to drink up your shame from that busted up cage.
I've been lost, sad and angry and full of rage.
But it's all the same cards shuffle up in this game.
Drink up all that poison before spitting it across the page.
Art isn't random it's born out of our pain.
Cutting ourselves on that sharp truth,
Like a curious child picks up a piece of broken glass.
The questions that go on inside one's mind and those we dare not ask.
Hidden behind layers of our youth where you're too afraid to find the real you.
A complex kind of buried truth.
Like a needle in a needle stack.
Afraid to stare in that rear-view mirror for fear of what's looking back?
That dark passenger we all have the one we think we lack.
With their tongue jammed in our ear whisper questions as they crave our constant feedback.

Yet still somehow, we try to act our best.
The trauma filled fruit laid out on the table for the judges to test.
But it all just goes to waste.
Demons want you to sin, so that they can have a taste.
The ones I couldn't face, even If I tried.
The ones that have had many lives, but sadly never died.
The ones that come with many names.
Where battles begun and guns were drawn but the bullets never came.
As I decide which road is best to take
Broken words or promises from friends that were sadly fake.
A pain staking reality, thoughts racing questions based upon our base morality.
Windows to the souls stained now with traumatised icing.
Nervous breakdown is the cherry on the cake for some of those that are baking.
Or the thorn pushed into the crown that some clowns were making.
Like betrayal hides amongst the crowd before we take it in.
Layers deep down hidden in pain sunken skin
Fighting to release the truth that's suffocating.
These poems are more like mirrors, as the pages form a maze.
Lost inside oneself looking for the answers whilst constantly in a daze.
Is this my discovery?
To finding all those missing pieces that will form the real me.

# YOUR INK

Your ink stains like no other
Tattooed to my heart and brain
With your stories of truthful courage,
A rainbow of relatable pain.
You paint graphic and haunting images
With your beautifully woven words.
Pin pricking every inch of my heart
With your honest and bravely written verse.
Your heart is a nest of poems ready to bleed onto every page.
Once read, they'll never leave us.
Beautifully scarred now.
Poems we'll take with us to our graves.

# NOT SURE WHAT TO SAY

This feeling of fear again not sure if my words will leave the pen.
That's swinging inside my head.
Ink dead perhaps or ideas lapsed.
Too much screen time has my mind collapsed.
Energy Zapped, perhaps.
I wonder how many poets can relate to this.
Staring at an empty page telling yourself to relax.
We bleed into every piece but our words are the oxygen that we all need.
Ideas that come to us like planting seeds.
But what happens when the inner critic tries to chop down trees?
How do we breathe art onto these pages?
If we can't focus on our metamorphic stages,
Cocooned by our own creativity,
Only to break out with wings singed from the flames of our own success and ability.
A pain we put on display instead of protecting our fragility.
Bursting through old skin as we try to find our way back in.
But being speechless isn't a sin.
So please don't pity me.
I don't want to fall into that pit you see,
Filled to the brim with despair where wondering eyes judge from the side.
Stripping away your armour till your left bare.
Like an exposed tooth that needs repair.
My mind like an empty cage no thoughts wish to visit this place.

Your only as good as your last piece or so your demons will have
you believe.
Writing is a gift and a curse and words are the worst when
they're not in a verse.
When they're playing hard to get.
Best lines ever have left to join the que of past regrets.
And yet I still squeeze at these thoughts.
Hoping to milk them for every word I can get.
But truth be told I need a word with myself.
This kind of behaviour isn't good for one's health.
Art is for the heart and not the head.
Analysing constantly words written or said,
Dissecting emotions from sentences like animals that are dead.
It just leaves me cut up.
Poetry is stories from the soul.
From those of us that have truly bled.

# WRITE THROUGH ME

Words fall from the sky landing on the page.
Helping us wade through some of our darkest days.
Now pages of pieces from our inner rage caged up like wild animals.
We can finally set them free.
Creating constellations with a mix of pain and poetry.
My hands surrender to my brains never ending story.
The words I'm truly grateful for that now flow **Write through me.**
My whole being becomes a vessel for words.
As they lovingly hijack my mind, body, and soul.
Stopping me in my tracks when they have something to say.
Or a poem to console.
Each verse is a blessing not a curse.
I don't mind my words whisking me far away.
Caught in the palms of paper
We write to set our pensive pains free and keep our demons at bay.
Poetry for me isn't the points we can score
It helps to keep the wolves from the door.
Cleaning out our caves of deep embedded misery as it brings a smile to the inner child in me.
Misspent time, on a misspent youth.
As the years swim by we finally discover our truth.
Pains we collect along the way like a detective gathering clues.
Never knowing the power, they hold.
Years later as we pick our way back through.
Poetry lives deep inside me and many of you.
The difference is we're the ones hanging on every word

Artistic outcasts perhaps, our love and passion seen as absurd.
Picking out every detail from our lives we willingly choose.
Soaking up every moment in time, not a single second to lose.
Pulling out our own heart strings to create relatable truths.
Poetry lives inside me my endless dark deep mystical sea.
Dancing through my blood
Fuelling my passion; helping to keep my mind demon free.
Painting with painful memories based on our reality.
I never feel betrayed by poetry
Because it's the one thing, that truly knows me.

# MARK MY WORDS

My words escape me as they fall from my mind.
Trying to transform into verse.
Stories aching from my heart I try to transcribe.
A gift given to some of us.
Imagine a world without words, a wordless universe.
Sometimes I find myself lost for words,
Which is ironic as it's a writer's curse.
But find a way to trust in our words.
Try to make sense with our art form we form sentences.
Pain is what we use to write with mostly these days.
Pens are no longer seen it's all done on keyboards
Or jotting down notes with the aid of our mobile screens.
Mind like a Scrabble board with a point system.
But what's the actual point if your words don't have true value.
Beyond where you place them.
We want them to leave the page and imprint on people's hearts
and brains.
Like a transfer or tattoo.
A moment we perhaps helped someone escape something dark
they were going through.
Or creating a bridge of relatability.
No one on this planet is demon free.
These words I spill are cheaper than any therapy.
Everything you read is a tiny part of me.
My soul in every word I pluck from the poet-tree.
Pain is my ink pot. My brain is the Quill.
Looking for a place to escape, your boredom I aim to kill.
Worried my creative well is running dry.
As I try to make sense of it all.
But poetry flows through me, freely, like a waterfall.

# BRUISED HALLWAYS
# AND BROKEN LOCKS

I don't write words to please the fans.
I write about the things going on in life I'm trying to
understand.
So many moments waisted on flavours that are bland.
I'm not doing this to create some kind of brand.
Poetry flows through me, and this is the kind of man I am.
A poet at heart and my art is where I stand.
So many drops of ink fall from the minds of many.
But only a small amount ever really lands.
Great ideas in the palm of our hands
That don't always make it into great stanzas
And that's something that I never understand.
Words are a tool that we use to carve out stories or feelings.
If they are just randomly placed because they sound nice then
what is their meaning?
Take me on a journey through your world.
Through a scared scarred reality with wounds as deep as oceans,
Pore them out for me.
I don't want to be teased with these pitter patter taps on the
surface
Break the seal and let me fall into that dark damaged hole.
Where demons eat the bones and leftovers of the good old days
As they're building up to feast on your soul.
Let me taste the way your life spills over sharp rocks
From harsh knocks and bruised hallways and broken locks
To doors that should remain locked.
Your words are the keys to those discoveries but sometimes you
get blocked.

Because you are too afraid to watch those words bleed across the page.
That's stained by the way you felt that day.
As your creative clock stops.
Hold on to those feelings that you've got.
This is a banquet for the soul, and I want to taste the lot.
Don't stop yourself halfway afraid of your plot.
Just see where those ink drops will take you.
Like think slots in casinos for the mind where you can find the big prize.
Your painful truth raw and flawed no longer hidden in disguise.
I'm in this place to be inspired daily.
I'm not a record so please don't try and play me.
But I will give you my best hits if you continue down this journey.
I'll leave you bruised by my truth maybe...

The way I see this world sometimes is enough to scare me.
But round so many corners are the onslaught of complainers
Word dictators and political makers that cause little earthquakes as they try to make this place shake us.
That dilute the passion and love and starts spreading haters.
I'm here for the poetry not the politics
That shit is the spoon for those that like to stir.
I'm just hear for the stories and words, not hear for mind games and harsh slurs.
This isn't a playground we are not kids now.
Put your swords down and pick up your pens now.
Leave your bulling days behind you,
Look in that mirror and ask yourself some harsh truths.
What are you here for?
And what can that pen of yours really do?
And so, I have my fill, and with these words I have I aim to kill.
The demons that swim through my mind as I drag them out with my quill.

I'm here to write about how this world makes me think.
And tell my stories with this pain fuelled ink.

# LOST POETRY LIST

Words inside my mind,
Jumbled up together like commuters on the jubilee line.
Words whizz bye like trains we've just missed.
Like a poet's album missing their greatest hits.
Some of our best work vanished swallowed up in that foggy
brain mist.
Swimming through thoughts desperately trying to think.
Spontaneous golden ideas slowly sink.
Pieces that gave us a lift, have now sank into the deep abyss.
A place where words and ideas go to die,
But nobody really knows why.
We yearn to bring them back but all we can do is try.
Empty spaces in our poems, now filled with the tear stains we
cried.
Moments of pure creation, taken in the blink of an eye.
Some of our best pieces will never be on display.
Some of our most powerful verses will never see the light of day.
Those words are a blank in a blanked-out space.
Like chalk marks around a cadaver souls taken without a trace.
Wonderful words we treasure the type that's impossible to re
place.
Hard to decipher the dashes and holes poems now looking more
like morse code.
We pray for those words to return.
But our minds keep saying no!
Where is it where all our missing words go?
They haunt our minds for days at a time,
Like missing children that we'll never find.
Words only there for a limited time.

We kill the ideas if we leave it too long.
A sensational sentence is now a Swan song.
The missing words we'll never find.
Somewhere out there, is a word graveyard lost in time.
Where poems come together,
A mix of Haikus, pros some even rhyme.
A place where the best poetry now lives.
I'm not sad my words were taken,
If they're joining the land of the lost poetry list.

# YOUR EVERY WORD

We can go days at a time without a single word.
Or conversations that rhyme.
As I embrace the hiatus because we'll be just fine.
When those words are whispered from your delicate lips
My mind is fully present with excitable fingertips.
I'm on the edge of my seat like I'm riding the precipice.
Doors that open dormant sores
Your words are weapons against those dark thoughts.
As I draw my sword every word leaves its mark where thoughts were caught.
Like dreams into weaved catchers, unseen yet be lieved.
Words are real magic hidden in minds not up magicians' sleeves.
Hearts and souls are the flowers, and your words are the bees.
Doing what you please, buzzing around our minds collecting thoughts like nectar.
Ideas growing wild like vines.
Like my heart is a page that wants to be stained with every emotion that was ever made.
To be explored like wild seas in the mind,
Where monsters and creatures of every kind are under the sur face.
Being able to see one's own truth and discovery.
You are what keeps my heart singing and soul glowing.
My all-knowing poetry.

Lightning Source UK Ltd.
Milton Keynes UK
UKHW010615240622
404905UK00002B/107

9 781800 689220